# ideals®
## THANKSGIVING

*More Than 50 Years of Celebrating Life's Most Treasured Moments*

Vol. 55, No. 5

*"O give thanks unto the Lord; for he is good;*
*for his mercy endureth for ever."*

—I Chronicles 16:34

Featured Photograph
12

Country Chronicle
16

Readers' Reflections
20

From My
Garden Journal
26

Bits & Pieces
30

Devotions
from the Heart
32

Remember When
38

Ideals'
Family Recipes
42

A Slice of Life
44

Legendary Americans
48

Our Heritage
52

Through My
Window
56

For the
Children
61

Handmade
Heirloom
64

Collector's
Corner
72

Traveler's
Diary
81

Readers' Forum
86

IDEALS—Vol. 55, No. 5 September MCMXCVIII IDEALS (ISSN 0019-137X) is published six times a year: January,
March, May, July, September, and November by IDEALS PUBLICATIONS INCORPORATED,
535 Metroplex Drive, Suite 250, Nashville, TN 37211.
Periodical postage paid at Nashville, Tennessee, and additional mailing offices.
Copyright © MCMXCVIII by IDEALS PUBLICATIONS INCORPORATED.
POSTMASTER: Send address changes to Ideals, PO Box 305300, Nashville, TN 37230. All rights reserved.
Title IDEALS registered U.S. Patent Office.

SINGLE ISSUE—U.S. $5.95 USD; Higher in Canada
ONE-YEAR SUBSCRIPTION—U.S. $19.95 USD; Canada $36.00 CDN (incl. GST and shipping); Foreign $25.95 USD
TWO-YEAR SUBSCRIPTION—U.S. $35.95 USD; Canada $66.50 CDN (incl. GST and shipping); Foreign $47.95 USD

ISBN 0-8249-1151-2   GST 131903775

# MERRY AUTUMN

It's all a farce, these tales they tell
  About the breezes sighing,
And moans astir o'er field and dell,
  Because the year is dying.

Such principles are most absurd,
  I care not who first taught 'em;
There's nothing known to beast or bird
  To make a solemn autumn.

In solemn times, when grief holds sway
  With countenance distressing,
You'll note the more of black and gray
  Will then be used in dressing.

Now purple tints are all around;
  The sky is blue and mellow;
And e'en the grasses turn the ground
  From modest green to yellow.

The seed burrs all with laughter crack
  On featherweed and jimson;
And leaves that should be
      dressed in black
  Are all decked out in crimson.

A butterfly goes winging by;
  A singing bird comes after;
And nature, all from earth to sky,
  Is bubbling o'er with laughter.

The ripples wimple on the rills,
  Like sparkling little lasses;
The sunlight runs along the hills
  And laughs among the grasses.

The earth is just so full of fun,
  It really can't contain it.
And streams of mirth so freely run;
  The heavens seem to rain it.

Don't talk to me of solemn days
  In autumn's time of splendor,
Because the sun shows fewer rays
  And these grow slant and slender.

Why, it's the climax of the year,—
  The highest time of living!—
Till naturally its bursting cheer
  Just melts into thanksgiving.

*Paul Laurence Dunbar*

*Autumn foliage brightens the landscape along the Carrabassett River in Maine. Photograph by Steve Terrill.*

# GIVE *ideals* THIS CHRISTMAS . . . .
# Let *ideals* express your heartfelt wishes at every season of the year!

WE'LL ANNOUNCE YOUR GIFTS WITH A HOLIDAY GREETING!

Every issue of *Ideals* is bursting with a celebration of life's special times: Christmas, Thanksgiving, Easter, Mother's Day, Country and Friendship. Give a gift subscription to *Ideals* this Christmas and you bring joy to the lives of special people six times a year! Each issue offers page after page of magnificent photographs, exquisite drawings and paintings, delightful stories and poetry. Each is a "keeper" that invites the reader back, again and again, to look and read and ponder. There's nothing quite as special as a gift of *Ideals*!

## SAVE 44%
### off the bookstore price!
### To order, mail card at right or call toll-free
# 1-800-558-4343

---

---

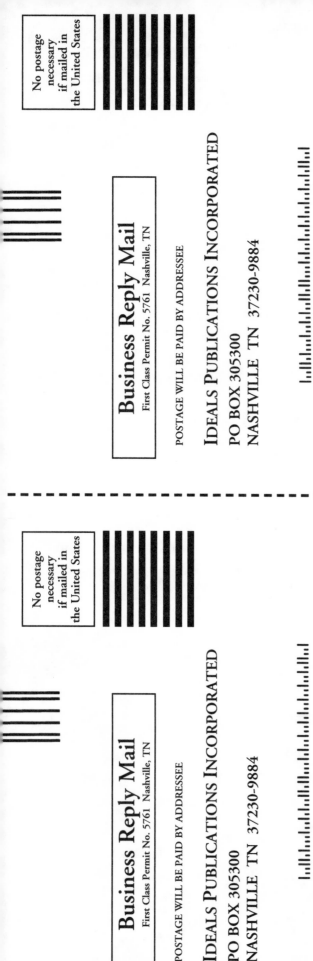

# *from* GREEN RIVER

When breezes are soft and skies are fair,
I steal an hour from study and care
and hie me away to the woodland scene
where wanders the stream with waters of green,
as if the bright fringe of herbs on its brink
had given their stain to the waves they drink;
and they, whose meadows it murmurs through,
have named the stream from its own fair hue.

That fairy music I never hear
nor gaze on those waters so green and clear
and mark them winding away from sight,
darkened with shade or flashing with light,
while o'er them the vine to its thicket clings
and the zephyr stoops to freshen his wings;
but I wish that fate had left me free
to wander these quiet haunts with thee,
till the eating cares of earth should depart,
and the peace of the scene pass into my heart;
and I envy thy stream, as it glides along
through its beautiful banks in a trance of song.

Though forced to drudge for the dregs of men
and scrawl strange words with the barbarous pen
and mingle among the jostling crowd,
where the sons of strife are subtle and loud—
I often come to this quiet place
to breathe the airs that ruffle thy face
and gaze upon thee in silent dream,
for in thy lonely and lovely stream
an image of that calm life appears
that won my heart in my greener years.

*William Cullen Bryant*

*The Pike River cascades down Eight Foot Falls in Twelve Foot Falls County Park,
Marinette County, Wisconsin. Photograph by Darryl R. Beers.*

# This Day

A newborn day! Oh, may I not
Leave on its shining page one blot
To mar its whiteness; may no tear
Of pity for myself appear
Upon it, or one low desire;
But ever turning love's flame higher
Within my breast, may I speak words
That lift the soul—like bright-winged birds—
And send them into skies of blue;
May all my thoughts be pure and true,
And everything I do today
Be done unselfishly; oh, may
I just forget myself and be
Helpful and kind and try to see
The good that is in everything,
And cause some weary heart to sing;
May I return the page tonight
To God—unspotted, clean and white.

Virginia Eaton

Normal day, let me be aware
of the treasure you are.
Let me learn from you,
love you, savor you, bless you
before you depart. Let me not
pass you by in quest of some rare
and perfect tomorrow.

Mary Jean Irion

*Morning light streams through the trees of Willamette National Forest in Oregon.
Photograph by Dennis Frates/Oregon Scenics.*

# THE SUMACH LEAVES

Some autumn leaves a painter took,
　　And with his colors caught their hues;
So true to nature did they look
　　That none to praise them could refuse.

The yellow mingling with the red
　　Shone beauteous in their bright decay,
And round a golden radiance shed,
　　Like that which hangs o'er parting day.

Their sister leaves, that, fair as these,
　　Thus far had shared a common lot,
All soiled and scattered by the breeze
　　Are now by every one forgot.

Soon, trodden under foot of men,
　　Their very forms will cease to be,
Nor they remembered be again,
　　Till Autumn decks once more the tree.

But these shall still their beauty boast,
　　To praise the painter's wondrous art,
When Autumn's glories all are lost
　　And with the fading year depart;

And through the wintry months so pale
　　The sumach's brilliant hues recall;
Where, waving over hill and vale,
　　They gave its splendor to our fall.

*Jones Very*

*Staghorn sumacs seem to set the roadways ablaze in Campton, New Hampshire.*
*Photograph by William Johnson/Johnson's Photography*

# COME, WALK WITH ME

Come, walk with me along the way
Where lanes are autumn-dressed.
Come, drink in all the colors fair,
And let your heart be blessed.

Come, see the flaming sumac plumes
Lift banners to the sky,
As goldenrod and asters nod
To us as we pass by.

Come, walk with me when leaves turn gold
And hills wear crimson hue,
Where pumpkins grow in amber fields
'Neath sky of matchless blue.

Come, walk with me this misty morn;
There's splendor to behold;
Along the country lanes we'll see
God's miracles unfold.

*Beverly J. Anderson*

# OCTOBER WEARS AN AMBER GOWN

When autumn's brightly patterned quilt
begins to fade and fray,
and corn abandons shriveled stalks
and fields are flaxen hay;

October stores her sunny clothes,
puts on an amber gown,
and scatters chestnut-colored leaves
along the roads to town.

She pauses by a peaceful pond
where children come to play,
but they're in school and fishes hide
in waters chilled and gray.

Alone, she hikes the woodland trails
through forests sere and still;
then slowly climbs in purple boots
up far November Hill.

*John C. Bonser*

*Sugar maples reflect the afternoon light in New Hampton, New Hampshire.*
*Photograph by William Johnson/Johnson's Photography.*

Seen from the Auferdeide National Scenic Byway in Oregon, the Roaring River tumbles through the

autumn-colored forest with glorious beauty. Photograph by Dennis Frates/Oregon Scenics.

# The Sheaves

Where long the shadows of the wind had rolled,
Green wheat was yielding to the change assigned;
And as by some vast magic undivined
The world was turning slowly into gold.
Like nothing that was ever bought or sold
It waited there, the body and the mind;
And with a mighty meaning of a kind
That tells the more the more it is not told.

So in a land where all days are not fair,
Fair days went on till on another day
A thousand golden sheaves were lying there,
Shining and still, but not for long to stay—
As if a thousand girls with golden hair
Might rise from where they slept and go away.

*Edwin Arlington Robinson*

*Artist Helen Allingham captures the innocence of yesteryear's farm girls napping among the sheaves.*
*Past Work, Helen Allingham. Christie's Images.*

# Country
# CHRONICLE
#### Lansing Christman

## Leaf Watching

Autumn leaves rarely wait for the first frost or freeze before they begin their soft tumbling. Some leaves fall gently and slowly; others as swift as a wing. Fallen leaves often litter my lawn in South Carolina before even a hint of frost breathes its cool breath over the Blue Ridge Mountains.

I always think of fallen leaves as autumn's leftovers. And they actually are. Fallen leaves are remnants of a year that saw them turn the trees to a springtime green. Remnants of a summer when the leaves spread their shade like a parasol over the dooryard grass. They are leftovers of the reds and scarlets and golds that painted the October hills in brilliant hues.

I prefer to be out-of-doors when the autumn leaves are falling, for I am fascinated by the manner in which they fall. I watch them in heavy rains when they join the sodden leaves already on the ground. I watch them on quiet days of sun when they fall in delicate spirals like feathers from the brilliant sky. Sometimes I detect a needle-like clicking song in the spiraling descent of dry, paper-like leaves—a song of autumn from crinkled forms touching one another on their float to earth.

There is excitement in watching leaves blown from trees in driving sheets on the wings of November's surging winds. They sweep and swirl across the lawn to rest at last in the shelter of hedges and fencerows, in ditches and deep ravines.

And I watch them skate. Not with the twists and turns of an Olympic skater, but I sometimes see them glide and turn their own kind of acrobatic somersaults.

The leaves fall. Autumn is closing the windows of the year. But this is just a moment in time; there is always that eternal hope—that looking ahead to the glorious green and flowering life of a new springtime just over the horizon.

---

*The author of two published books, Lansing Christman has been contributing to* Ideals *for more than twenty years. Mr. Christman has also been published in several American, foreign, and braille anthologies. He lives in rural South Carolina.*

*Ivy intertwines between colorful maple leaves in the Washington Park Arboretum of Seattle, Washington. Photograph by Terry Donnelly.*

# AUTUMN IN TENNESSEE

This is the season when the colors glow,
Splashed vividly in prodigality
Across the mountains and the high plateau,
In autumn's masterpiece of tapestry.

Gold hickories and flaming maples thread
Their looms  near pine and cedar greens, while oaks,
Dogwoods, and sweetgums weave patterns of red,
With crimson sumacs adding lavish strokes.

Oh, I must find a day—and soon—to go
And see again an autumn's gold sunrise
Upon these mountains.  I have lived to know
What peace the heart may garner through the eyes.

*Isla Paschal Richardson*

*The foothills of the Smoky Mountains near Gatlinburg, Tennessee,
burst into October color. Photograph by Ken Dequaine.*

# Readers' Reflections

*Editor's Note: Readers are invited to submit unpublished, original poetry for possible publication in future issues of Ideals. Please send typed copies only; manuscripts will not be returned. Writers receive $10 for each published submission. Send material to Readers' Reflections, Ideals Publications Inc., P.O. Box 305300, Nashville, Tennessee 37230-5300.*

## THE RED WHEELBARROW

In a ditch in the country,
   while taking a ride,
I see a red wheelbarrow
   propped on its side.
The wheel is all rusty,
   the handles broke free,
but it looks like a chariot
   waiting for me.
My hands on the wheel
   shake as memories loom
of a long-ago time
   on a fall afternoon.
I can see the leaves falling
   as tears of today
when I think of how brother
   turned work into play.
Our red wheelbarrow was heaped
   high with leaves

and limbs that had dropped
   from the red maple trees.
I can smell the woodsmoke
   as strong arms lift me high
and I plop in the wheelbarrow,
   face to the sky.
I still laugh in wonder
   as I call to mind
how that wheelbarrow flew
   with big brother behind.
Well, I've ridden in autos,
   in ships and in trains,
raced in a motorboat,
   flew in jet planes.
But I've never felt such
   a marvelous thrill
as when that red wheelbarrow
   flew down the hill.

*Ruth Roberts Douglas*
*Williston, Florida*

## AUTUMN

Vivid colors dress the trees
    My favorite time of year,
Golden fields against a sky
    Intensely blue and clear.

Morning sun that warms my heart,
    At night, the harvest moon.
Beauty shines from everywhere;
    It's over all too soon.

Stay awhile, my season friend;
    Don't let your presence fade.
Winter veils you swiftly now
    To show your song has played.

*Dema Opal Draper Matteson*
*Three Rivers, Michigan*

## OCTOBER

Hot, dry October winds
Swoop down and blow
Dried brown leaves
Into dusty funnel clouds
To set the autumn stage—
A cast of thousands
Like the flocks of blackbirds
That undulate in the sky
Up and down
Between oak and maple
On the same wind
That billows the tablecloth
Spread by picnickers
On one last outing.

*Jan Harvey*
*Sumner, Iowa*

## TRANSITION

Leaves rustle underneath our feet;
    Autumnal colors flood the scene—
A mass of varicolored hues,
    In shades of orange, and gold, and green.

The scent of fall is in the air;
    Old Jack Frost is drawing near.
Dying leaves dance in the wind,
    Their last hurrah with us to share.

The harvest moon keeps shining bright
    And bids farewell to autumn's glow.
The wintertime comes rushing in
    With the elegance of falling snow.

*Barbara Cagle Ray*
*Nashville, Tennessee*

## BLACKBIRDS

My yard is black with birds today,
    they're scratching in a flurry.
They hope to find a lot of worms
    because they're in a hurry.

I reach to get my camera
    to catch this lovely scene,
but when I turn to focus
    not a blackbird can be seen.

*Armavena Leigh Buckmaster*
*Dumas, Texas*

# October

Late summer thrives although the woods
Are filled with Winter's prophecy
In thinning leaves and russet tones
Of red and yellow tracery.

Still morning boasts the song of birds
And night is routed gallantly.
But twilight hears the cricket's call
With rhythmic, shrill insistency.

Now from the woods new voices come—
The "owl complaining to the moon"—
And echoing through the leafy vault,
The eerie laughter of the loon.

Thin frost upon the meadow land,
A trail of birds across the sky,
A keenness in the vibrant air
That sends the dead leaves whirling by.

*Josephine Powell Beaty*

*Huckleberry bushes in autumn color nestle
among the beargrass in Waldo Lake Wilderness,
Willamette National Forest, Oregon.
Photograph by Steve Terrill.*

~22~

# AUTUMN'S GOLDEN HOUR

Walk quietly here—
Lest birds be stirred to flight
By sound of feet
Upon the russet leaves
Along the garden path.

Walk slowly—
Lest you miss the beauty
Of this golden hour
That soon will purple
Beneath autumn skies.

Walk gently—
While life becomes imbued
With nature's riches
And hopes that once were only dreams
Lie warm upon the heart.

*May Smith White*

Aspen trees rain a golden shower of leaves along Glacier Creek Trail
in Rocky Mountain National Park, Colorado. Photograph by Mary Liz Austin.

# From My
# Garden Journal
### by Deana Deck

## BITTERSWEET

Bittersweet. The word calls to mind old memories, lost loves, missed opportunities—pleasures mingled with regrets. Or maybe it just reminds you of the delightfully offbeat taste of semi-sweet chocolate. To clothing designers and advertising copywriters, of course, bittersweet simply represents a creative way of identifying a subdued orange color.

To gardeners, however, bittersweet is a glorious climbing vine. Bittersweet makes a wonderful addition to the landscape because of its colorful autumn fruit, but the plant can have an aggressive nature. Gardeners well know that the pleasure of bittersweet's beauty can come mingled with the regret of rampant and unwanted invasion.

There are two related species: *Celastrus orbiculatus*,

the Oriental bittersweet, and *C. scandens*, the American bittersweet. The celastrus vine is easy to grow. It thrives in sun or shade and is not at all particular about the soil in which it is planted. The leaves turn soft yellow in fall and the vine bears abundant fruit, each about the size of a pea. When it first forms, the fruit is a pale green, then matures into yellow, papery fruit cases that burst when ripe to reveal brilliant orange-red seeds against a yellow background. Since birds do not seem interested in devouring the seeds, they will remain on the vine long into winter and bring a bright splash of color to the winter landscape.

Bittersweet requires almost no care and, in fact, can often be spotted growing untended along the roadside, winding itself up the nearest tree and strangling it to death, since that is the bittersweet nature of this twining vine. Keeping a bittersweet vine under control can be a challenge because it tends to spread roots underground that appear in unwanted locations. In the classic Victorian language of flowers, bittersweet signifies "Truth;" the truth about bittersweet is that, given the least opportunity, it would very likely take over your entire garden.

Northern gardeners have an easier time controlling bittersweet than do gardeners in the South, because hard winters

BITTERSWEET

tend to slow the vine's growth. Bittersweet, however, can be kept under control with diligence. Pruning yearly will not only help keep the vine from becoming invasive, but it will also result in more abundant production of the attractive fruit.

Another method of controlling bittersweet is to root prune it. The best way to do this is by digging straight down in a circle around the plant with a sharp spade to cut the roots and prevent spreading.

A mature bittersweet vine is worth the effort required to keep it under control. It can reach lengths of thirty or forty feet as it twines its way upward in the nearest tree; and in the fall and winter, it displays spectacular color. A sturdy cedar arbor is one of the best places for bittersweet to climb because it cannot only damage trees as it twines around the trunk and branches, but it can also kill young trees by blocking out the sun with its foliage. By planting bittersweet at the base of an arbor, you can keep the plant pruned to encourage thicker foliage and more fruit.

The berries of the bittersweet vine are wonderful additions to autumn flower arrangements and can be used to create a colorful and unusual centerpiece for the Thanksgiving table. An informal arrangement of fresh chrysanthemums and asters contrasts nicely with dried ornamental grasses and miniature pumpkins or small gourds to provide the perfect background for dried bunches of brilliant, orange-red bittersweet berries.

No special talent is required to dry bittersweet berries, just pick them at their peak of color and freshness. Dry the berries by hanging them with twine or by standing berry-laden branches upright in containers. Filling the bottom of the container with an inch or so of water will permit the bittersweet berries to dry slowly as the water evaporates; when dried by this technique, the berries will retain more of their original color and form.

Although the glorious bittersweet vine may indeed provide a bittersweet experience, the pleasure you will derive from the bright, colorful berries each autumn will far outweigh the mild regret you may experience in spring while you prune away its unwanted offspring.

*By planting bittersweet at the base of an arbor, you can also keep the plant pruned to encourage thicker foliage and more fruit.*

*Deana Deck tends her flowers, plants, and vegetables at her home in Nashville, Tennessee, where her popular garden column is a regular feature in* The Tennessean.

# THE FESTIVAL OF PRAISE

What can we sing to One whose verse
    Eternal song unbars?
What give to Him whose cloud-fringed purse
    Is crammed with gleaming stars?
A doubly pious way consists,
    When we our thanks would bring,
In recollecting He exists
    In every living thing;
That when of beast or man we touch
    With pity-helping care,
'Tis known in heaven just as much
    As if we did it there;
That when our voice in kind behalf
    Of any grief is heard,
Heaven's wondrous gold-foiled phonograph
    Is taking every word;
That when a heart the earth-heart serves,
    Of diamond or clod,
It thrills the universe's nerves,
    And glads the soul of God.

*Will Carleton*

*American artist Jane Wooster Scott brings to life a
Thanksgiving church service in* Command Performance.
*Jane Wooster Scott/Superstock.*

# BITS & PIECES

The October day is a dream,
bright and beautiful as the rainbow,
and as brief and fugitive.
        W. Hamilton Gibson

Poems are made by fools like me,
But only God can make a tree.
        Joyce Kilmer

The tree is full of poetry.
        Henry David Thoreau

There is a beautiful spirit breathing now
Its mellow richness on the clustered trees,
And, from a beaker full of richest dyes,
Pouring new glory on the autumn woods,
And dripping in warm light the pillared clouds.
        Henry Wadsworth Longfellow

O world, as God has made it!
All is beauty.
Robert Browning

Unto thee, O God, do we give thanks,
unto thee do we give thanks: for that thy
name is near thy wondrous works declare.
Psalm 75:1

Each moment of the year has its own beauty . . .
a picture which was never seen before and which
shall never be seen again.

Ralph Waldo Emerson

In heaven it is always autumn.
His mercies are ever in their maturity.
John Donne

But see the fading many-colored woods,
Shade deep'ning over shade, the country round
Imbrown; crowded umbrage, dusk and dun
Of every hue, from wan-declining green
To sooty dark.

James Thomson

# Devotions FROM THE Heart

Pamela Kennedy

*As ye have therefore received Christ Jesus the Lord, so walk ye in him: Rooted and built up in him, and stablished in the faith, as ye have been taught, abounding therein with thanksgiving.*

*Colossians 2:6–7*

## LIVING THANKSGIVING

From their earliest days, I taught my children to say "thank you" when they received something. Good manners required it. Saying "thank you" was the proper thing to do. Before long the words popped out of their mouths with regularity and, as with most habits, little thought. When they were old enough to print, we moved on to thank you notes. These were required to be written before a gift could be enjoyed (good manners again). My intent was for my children to incorporate the giving of thanks as a lifestyle, but often they viewed the inevitable thank-you note as a chore and the thankful sentiments on the note seldom reflected heartfelt gratitude. Just a few days ago I was leafing through a book catalog and saw an advertisement for a book claiming to contain "just the right words" for any situation, from thank-you notes to condolences. I wondered if these all-purpose sentiments would be as those of my reluctant children.

Whereas our spoken and written words are certainly important, perhaps a more meaningful expression of thanks is to live in such a way that our actions and attitudes reflect the gratitude in our hearts. There are many beautiful examples of this kind of living thanksgiving found in the pages of the Bible. King Solomon built the greatest temple Israel ever knew as an offering of thanksgiving to God. This magnificent structure was looted and destroyed by conquering invaders; but over four hundred years later, the prophet Ezra supervised a rebuilding effort that resulted in a second temple.

*Dear Father, I thank you for the abundant blessings you give me every day. Help me to translate my gratitude into a lifestyle of thanksgiving, passing your blessings along to others. Amen.*

Although Ezra's temple lacked the beauty and grandeur of Solomon's, the motivation for its construction was the same; and when the re-gathered people of Israel laid the foundation, Scriptures tell us they sang to God with praise and thanksgiving (Ezra 3:11). In the pages of the gospels we read of a poverty-stricken outcast who learned that Jesus was dining with a Pharisee. She risked all she had to enter the wealthy man's home, anoint the Lord with perfume, wash his feet with her tears, and dry them with her hair. And what was her motivation? Jesus said it was gratitude (Luke 7:36–50).

These examples of thanksgiving go far beyond the spoken or written word. They are living thank-you notes scripted in acts of devotion and compassion. How would our lives and those around us be changed if we began living our thanksgiving? We might not be able to build a grand temple, but we can build hope in others by lending a hand when they are in need. We can donate time, money, or expertise to projects that train people to rebuild their own lives. We cannot minister to Jesus directly, but hasn't he said whatever we do for the least of his children, we do for Him? In His name we can wipe away the tears of a frightened child or pour the perfume of kindness on someone in despair. We can listen to one who is lonely and hold the hand of one in grief.

There is no need to limit our thank yous to notes and phone calls. When we allow gratitude for what God had done for us to spill over into the lives of others we become examples of living thanksgiving.

*A church steeple peeks through the trees in Waitsfield, Vermont. Photograph by Ed Harp/Unicorn Stock Photos.*

# Sign Posts

I have not voiced profound, deep truths,
Nor lived them as I've wanted to,
Not having glimpsed infinity;
My groping fingertips but touched
The fringes of reality;
My own uncertain, wavering steps
Not ones to follow. But could I
Leave sign posts somewhere on the way—
Sign posts for young and eager feet—
Pointing to beckoning splendor-trails,
I think that looking back I'd know
A deep contentment if some eyes
Were thus alerted to behold
The grandeur and simplicity
Of earthly beauty here and now.

*Isla Paschal Richardson*

# Child of the Open

Child of the open am I, am I,
Child of the earth and the boundless sky,
Born of the sunrise, when heaven rests
Just for the moment upon earth's breast.

That's why my wandering soul will be
Ever a part of the earth, and free,
Free as the wind on the cloud-swept heights,
Wild as the waves through the starless nights.

Child of the open with earth-bound feet
Tripping along a celestial street,
Reaching the crest but to fall and rise,
Seeking the point where a balance lies.

Earth in her infinite way rolls on—
Out of the darkness is born the dawn.
Child of the open am I, am I,
Child of the earth and the boundless sky.

*Mary E. Linton*

*A little girl stops from her play to admire her favorite fallen leaf. Photograph by Kotoh/Zefa/H. Armstrong Roberts.*
*A pumpkin picker picks the perfect pumpkin at Sunny Acres Farm in West Chicago, Illinois. Photograph by Jim Whitmer.*
*Father and son practice riding a bicycle among the soft cushion of autumn leaves. Photograph by D. Degnan/H. Armstrong Roberts.*

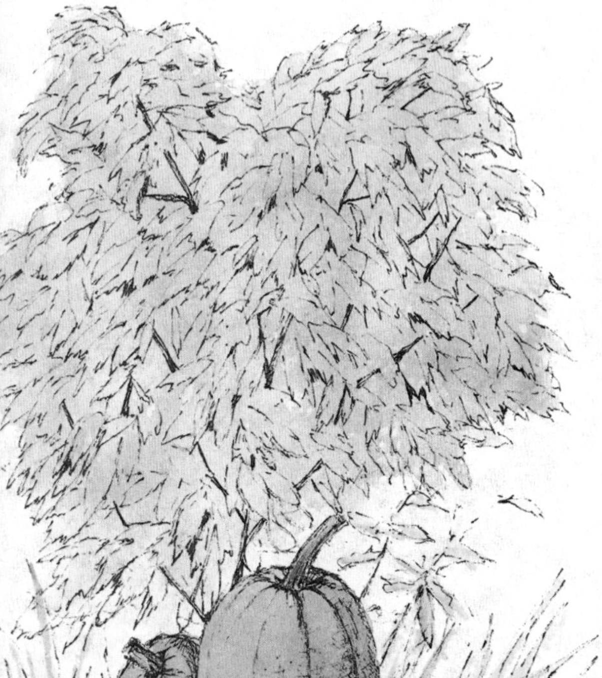

# BY STILL WATERS

*. . . He leadeth me beside the still waters; he restoreth my soul.*

*Psalm 23:2–3*

My tent stands in a garden
    Of aster and goldenrod,
Tilled by the rain and the sunshine,
    And sown by the hand of God—
An old New England pasture
    Abandoned to peace and time,
And by the magic of beauty
    Reclaimed to the sublime.

About it are golden woodlands
    Of tulip and hickory;
On the open ridge behind it
    You may mount to a glimpse of sea—
The far-off, blue, Homeric
    Rim of the world's great shield,
A border of boundless glamor
    For the soul's familiar field.

In purple and gray-wrought lichen
    The boulders lie in the sun;
Along its grassy footpath
    The white-tailed rabbits run.
The crickets work and chirrup
    Through the still afternoon;
And the owl calls from the hillside
    Under the frosty moon.

The odorous wild grape clambers
    Over the tumbling wall,
And through the autumnal quiet
    The chestnuts open and fall.
Sharing time's freshness and fragrance,
    Part of the earth's great soul,
Here man's spirit may ripen
    To wisdom serene and whole.

Shall we not grow with the asters—
    Never reluctant nor sad,
Not counting the cost of being,
    Living to dare and be glad?
Shall we not lift with the crickets
    A chorus of ready cheer,
Braving the frost of oblivion,
    Quick to be happy here?

Is my will as sweet as the wild grape,
    Spreading delight on the air
For the passer-by's enchantment,
    Subtle and unaware?
Have I as brave a spirit,
    Sprung from the self-same mould,
As this weed from its own contentment
    Lifting its shaft of gold?

*Multi-colored trees reflect in the Reuben Hart Reservoir in the Litchfield Hills area of Connecticut. Photograph by William Johnson/Johnson's Photography.*

The deep red cones of the sumach
    And the woodbine's crimson's sprays
Have bannered the common roadside
    For the pageant of passing days.
These are the oracles Nature
    Fills with her holy breath,
Giving them glory of color,
    Transcending the shadow of death.

Here in the sifted sunlight
    A spirit seems to brood
On the beauty and worth of being,
    In tranquil, instinctive mood;
And the heart, filled full of gladness
    Such as the wise earth knows,
Wells with a full thanksgiving
    For the gifts that life bestows:

For the ancient and virile nurture
    Of the teeming primordial ground,
For the splendid gospel of color,
    The rapt revelations of sound;
For the morning-blue above us
    And the rusted gold of the fern,
For the chickadee's call to valor
Bidding the faint-heart turn;

For fire and running water,
    Snowfall and summer rain;
For sunsets and quiet meadows,
    The fruit and standing grain;

For the solemn hour of moonrise
    Over the crest of trees,
When the mellow lights are kindled
    In the lamps of the centuries;

For those who wrought aforetime,
    Led by the mystic strain
To strive for the larger freedom,
    And live for the greater gain;
For plenty and peace and playtime,
    The homely goods of earth,
And for rare immaterial treasures
    Accounted of little worth;

For art and learning and friendship,
    Where beneficent truth is supreme,—
Those everlasting cities
    Built on the hills of dream;
For all things growing and goodly
    That foster this life, and breed
The immortal flower of wisdom
    Out of the mortal seed.

But most of all for the spirit
    That cannot rest nor bide
In stale and sterile convenience,
    Nor safely proven and tried,
But still inspired and driven,
    Must seek what better may be,
And up from the loveliest garden
    Must climb for a glimpse of sea.

*Bliss Carman*

# Remember When

## SUPPER'S READY!

From *You and I and Yesterday* by Marjorie Holmes

Whatever happened to the family dinner hour? Or "supper" as we called it in our small town? That time at the end of the day when everybody was summoned to wash up and sit down together to share a common meal. A time not only to eat but to talk to each other, even if you sometimes quarreled. A time and place where you could laugh, joke, exchange ideas, tell stories, dump your troubles. (Yes, and learn your manners.). . .

"Suppertime!" The last meal of the day. . . .

Only city folks or people who put on city airs called it dinner. To us dinner was at noon, and we didn't mean lunch, we meant *dinner*. When we spoke of three square meals a day we meant three square meals. During

the morning, along with everything else she had to do, a woman was also getting dinner. Tending the pot roast or pounding the beefsteak, cooking the vegetables and potatoes, making a custard and opening a Mason jar of pears or home-canned applesauce. And promptly on the stroke of twelve it had to be ready. For at that point the town's activities would come to a sudden halt with the blasting of the noon whistle at the firehouse.

On that instant stores and offices closed, school got out. A few doctors and lawyers and businessmen ate at Martin's Cafe or the Bradford Hotel, but most men headed for home. Since we had no school cafeterias or buses we walked home too—only the country kids, whom we envied, were allowed to bring their lunches. Winter or spring, fair weather or foul, we walked; and since our house was more than a mile away, it was stow away all that food and start back so you wouldn't be late. (To be tardy was a disgrace.) Anyway, noon dinner in our town was an hour of suspended activity, except for a sense of clicking dishes and earnestly munching jaws.

Supper was different. More leisurely. Less a time of common refueling than an hour when everybody gathered at the day's end to summarize and share what had gone on. And it varied with families. You'd begin to hear the calls, "Hey kids, come on now, time to help get supper—" or the announcement, "Supper's ready!" all over the neighborhood anywhere from five o'clock on. People like the Renshaws ate early; Mr. Renshaw worked the night shift at the creamery and liked a long evening with his family before he donned his white overalls and departed. . . . Mrs. Flanders who liked to gad and was sort of slapdash about her cooking never managed to round up her brood until nearly seven o'clock—to the horror of some women and the distress of many kids, because most of us had finished the dishes by then and were ready to play out again. . . .

But whatever we ate for supper, whether the fare was feast or famine, certain rules prevailed: The whole family ate in the dining room, on a linen cloth with linen napkins. Nobody ever sat down before Mother. And nobody ever left the table unless she excused him first. Nor did we ever begin until everyone was present and until the blessing was asked. Also, we all had to sit straight in our chairs, left hand in the lap. No reaching, no stooping or slurping, and every request prefaced by "please." Mother believed in the old saw: "Always eat as if you were dining with the king, then you'll never be embarrassed if the king comes to dine."

# Thanksgiving

My heart gives thanks for many things;
  For strength to labor day by day,
For sleep that comes when darkness wings
  With evening up the eastern way.
I give deep thanks that I'm at peace
  With kith and kin and neighbors, too—
Dear Lord, for all last year's increase,
  That helped me strive and hope and do.

My heart gives thanks for many things;
  I know not how to name them all.
My soul is free from frets and stings,
  My mind from creed and doctrine's thrall.
For sun and stars, for flowers and streams,
  For work and hope and rest and play—
For empty moments given to dreams,
  For these my heart gives thanks today.

William Stanley Braithwaite

*F*or three things I thank God every
day of my life: thanks that He has
vouchsafed me knowledge of His works;
deep thanks that He has set in my
darkness the lamp of faith; deep, deep-
est thanks that I have another life to
look forward to—a life joyous with
light and flowers and heavenly song.

Helen Adams Keller

A mossy bigleaf maple shades the Wildwood Chapel in the Skagit River Valley of Skagit County, Washington. Photograph by Terry Donnelly.

Pototschnik

# Ideals' Family Recipes

## Sweet Potato Soufflé

One 18-ounce can sweet potatoes, drained
1 cup granulated sugar
2 eggs
½ cup milk
½ teaspoon salt
⅓ stick butter or margarine, melted

1 teaspoon vanilla
Topping:
1 cup light brown sugar, packed
½ cup all-purpose flour
1 cup chopped pecans
⅓ cup melted butter or margarine

Preheat oven to 350° F. In a large bowl, mash sweet potatoes until smooth. Add granulated sugar, eggs, milk, salt, melted butter or margarine, and vanilla; mix well. Pour mixture into a two-quart buttered baking dish; set aside.

In a separate mixing bowl, combine light brown sugar, flour, and chopped pecans. Add melted butter or margarine and mix well. Crumble topping over potato mixture. Bake uncovered 35 to 45 minutes. Serve warm. Makes 10 to 12 servings.

*Marian Schultz*
*Sturgeon Bay, Wisconsin*

## Double Layer Pumpkin Dessert

One 8-inch prepared graham cracker pie crust
3 ounces cream cheese, softened
1 tablespoon granulated sugar
1 cup plus 1 tablespoon cold milk
1½ cups frozen non-dairy whipped topping, thawed

Two 3.4-ounce packages instant vanilla pudding
1 teaspoon ground cinnamon
½ teaspoon ground ginger
¼ teaspoon ground cloves
One 15-ounce can pumpkin

In a large bowl, combine softened cream cheese, granulated sugar, and 1 tablespoon of the cold milk; beat with an electric mixer until smooth. Fold in non-dairy whipped topping. Spread mixture over pie crust.

In a separate bowl, combine the remaining cold milk, pudding mix, spices, and pumpkin. Beat with an electric mixer until well blended (mixture will be thick). Spread over cream cheese layer in graham cracker pie crust. Chill 4 hours or until set. Makes 2 pies.

*Marie Rossey*
*Creston, Ohio*

## Fresh Apple Harvest Cake

4 cups peeled, cored, and chopped apples
3 cups all-purpose flour
1 teaspoon baking soda
1 teaspoon salt
1 teaspoon ground cinnamon
3 eggs
2 cups granulated sugar

1½ cups vegetable oil
1 teaspoon vanilla
1 cup coarsely chopped walnuts or pecans
Topping:
1 cup light brown sugar, packed
1 stick (⅓ cup) butter
¼ cup evaporated milk

Preheat oven to 350° F. Grease and flour a 13- x 9- x 2-inch baking pan. Prepare apples and set aside. In a medium bowl, sift together flour, baking soda, salt, and cinnamon; set aside. In a large bowl, beat eggs; add granulated sugar and mix well. Stir in oil and vanilla, mixing well. Add sifted dry ingredients gradually, stirring well after each addition. Fold in chopped apples and nuts. Spoon batter into pan. Bake 45 minutes or until toothpick inserted in center comes out clean. Remove to wire rack.

In a small saucepan, combine light brown sugar, butter, and evaporated milk. Cook over medium heat for 5 minutes, stirring constantly. Pour glaze over hot cake. Serve warm. Makes 12 to 15 servings.

*Nancy Grady Wilson*
*Kenansville, North Carolina*

## Cranberry Cream Pie

Two 8-inch prepared graham cracker pie crusts
One 8-ounce package cream cheese, softened
One 14-ounce can sweetened condensed milk
½ cup plus ¼ cup frozen cranberry juice cocktail concentrate, thawed

2 tablespoons lemon juice
One 8-ounce container non-dairy whipped topping, thawed
One 16-ounce can whole berry cranberry sauce
1 tablespoon cornstarch

In a large bowl, beat softened cream cheese until fluffy. Gradually beat in sweetened condensed milk until smooth. Add ½ cup of the cranberry juice concentrate and lemon juice; mix well. Fold in non-dairy whipped topping. Divide mixture between graham cracker pie crusts; chill 3 hours or until set.

In a medium saucepan, combine whole berry cranberry sauce, ¼ cup of the thawed juice concentrate, and cornstarch. Over medium heat, cook mixture, stirring constantly, until it reaches a boil; remove from heat. Refrigerate to thoroughly chill. Spoon chilled cranberry topping over pies. Makes 8 to 10 servings.

*Jan Hoffbauer*
*Tiffin, Ohio*

# A SLICE OF LIFE

— Edgar A. Guest —

## THE OLD-FASHIONED THANKSGIVING

It may be I am getting old
    And like too much to dwell
Upon the days of bygone years,
    The days I loved so well;
But thinking of them now I wish
    Somehow that I could know
A simple old Thanksgiving Day,
    Like those of long ago,
When all the family gathered round
    A table richly spread,
With little Jamie at the foot
    And Grandpa at the head,
The youngest of us all to greet
    The oldest with a smile,
With Mother running in and out
    And laughing all the while.

It may be I'm old-fashioned,
    But it seems to me today
We're too much bent on having fun
    To take the time to pray;
Each little family grows up with
    Fashions of its own;
It lives within a world itself
    And wants to be alone.
It has its special pleasures,
    Its circle, too, of friends;
There are no get-together days;
    Each one his journey wends,
Pursuing what he likes the best
    In his particular way,
Letting the others do the same
    Upon Thanksgiving Day.

I like the olden way the best,
    When relatives were glad
To meet the way they used to do
    When I was but a lad;
The old home was a rendezvous
    For all our kith and kin,
And whether living far or near
    They all came trooping in
With shouts of "Hello, Daddy!"
    As they fairly stormed the place
And made a rush for Mother,
    Who would stop to wipe her face
Upon her gingham apron
    Before she kissed them all,
Hugging them proudly to her breast,
    The grown-ups and the small.

Then laughter rang throughout the home, and,
    Oh, the jokes they told;
From Boston, Frank brought new ones,
    but Father sprang the old;
All afternoon we chatted,
    telling what we hoped to do
The struggles we were making
    and the hardships we'd gone through;
We gathered round the fireside.
    How fast the hours would fly.
It seemed before we'd settled down
    'twas time to say goodbye.
Those were the glad Thanksgivings,
    the old-time families knew
When relatives could still be friends
    and every heart was true.

---

*Edgar A. Guest began his illustrious career in 1895 at the age of fourteen when his work first appeared in the* Detroit Free Press. *His column was syndicated in over three hundred newspapers, and he became known as "The Poet of the People."*

---

*Patrick McRae is an artist who lives in New Berlin, Wisconsin. He has created nostalgic artwork for* Ideals *for more than a decade, and his favorite models are his wife and three children.*

# FIRE DREAMS

*(Written to be read aloud, if so be, Thanksgiving Day)*

I remember here by the fire,
In the flickering reds and saffrons,
They came in a ramshuckle tub,
Pilgrims in tall hats,
Pilgrims of iron jaws,
Drifting by weeks on beaten seas,
And the random chapters say
They were glad and sang to God.

And so
Since the iron-jawed men sat down
And said, "Thanks, O God,"
For life and soup and a little less
Than a hobo handout today,
Since gray winds blew gray patterns of sleet on Plymouth Rock,
Since the iron-jawed men sang "Thanks, O God,"
You and I, O Child of the West,
Remember more than ever
November and the hunter's moon,
November and the yellow-spotted hills.

And so
In the name of the iron-jawed men
I will stand up and say yes till the finish is come and gone.
God of all broken hearts, empty hands, sleeping soldiers,
God of all star-flung beaches of night sky,
I and my love-child stand up together to-day and sing:
"Thanks, O God."

*Carl Sandburg*

A roaring fire welcomes visitors to a cozy winter cottage. Photograph by S. Barth/H. Armstrong Roberts.

## SOJOURNER TRUTH

By the first light of the morning on June 1, 1843, a forty-six-year-old American woman by the name of Isabella stepped off the ferry in Brooklyn, New York, and began walking eastward toward Long Island. Behind her was a life filled with pain and hardship. Isabella had been born a slave and lived almost thirty years in bondage. For the decade and a half that followed her emancipation, her family, scattered and scarred by slavery, and her world constrained by prejudice, she struggled to make a life for herself in New York City. But on this June morning, Isabella was full of hope. Powered by faith, she had given herself the new name of Sojourner Truth and had resolved to walk out into the world and preach the word of God and the love of Jesus Christ.

Sojourner Truth walked eastward across Long Island, then on into Connecticut, and northward into Massachusetts. Along the way she spoke to individuals, to camp meetings, to church groups, to anyone who would pause long enough to listen. She was tall and strong-bodied, a bold and outspoken black woman whose mere physical presence drew attention and whose words could hold listeners rapt. But it was not until her journey took her into the town of Northampton, Massachusetts, that America took real notice of Sojourner Truth and the powerful message of her life began to be heard.

In Northampton, a group of men and women had founded a utopian society devoted to the causes of abolition and women's rights. Their approach was passionate, but often intellectual, and the society tended to view the two causes—abolition and women's rights—as entirely separate crusades. Abolition was considered a male issue, whereas the issue of women's rights was considered the sole domain of white, upper-class women. When Sojourner Truth walked into their midst, they saw their two causes dovetail: here was a former slave who had known the brutality of forced servitude and a woman who had known the feeling of being invisible and insignificant in a male-dominated world.

Under the influence of the Northampton community, which at times included William Lloyd Garrison and Frederick Douglass, Sojourner Truth began speaking about abolition and about the oppression of women. She drew from her life experiences to document the harsh, inhumane life of the slave, and presented herself—a far cry from the refined, upper-class white women who made up the greater part of the nascent women's rights movement in America—as undeniable proof that this cause must embrace women of all races and social classes. She told her audiences about watching her parents suffer the results of long hard lives of servitude, about having siblings sold away from the family, about bearing five children of her own into lives of bondage. She moved and shocked those who heard her, and for those willing to hear the truth of her message, she revealed the cruel realities of life in nineteenth-century America. At an Ohio women's rights convention in 1851, Sojourner Truth asked repeatedly, "Ain't I a woman?" Her question forced the issue—one must stand for an equality blind to differences in color and gender and social class: anything less, and one served the side of the oppressors.

In her long, hard life, Sojourner Truth grew from a compliant slave girl who never thought to question her lot in life to a speaker renowned enough to be an invited guest at Abraham Lincoln's White House. With her voice and her passion she inspired many Americans to the cause of abolition, opened many eyes to the oppression of most women in America, and, after slavery was made illegal, kept on speaking and working to convince white Americans to accept freed black slaves as equal members of their society. But the most important day of her life came long before the public knew her name, long before she had even taken on that name. In 1826, the slave Isabella, only months shy of her thirtieth birthday, stood up one morning and walked away—away from her master's farm, away forever from her life as a slave. In truth, New York law was set to free her the following year. But on that morning Isabella decided not to accept that her freedom was a matter for the law to decide. On the day she walked away from her life in bondage, she defied the master who held her in slavery to serve the Lord, and she freed herself to live a life in service to humanity.

> *At an Ohio women's rights convention in 1851, Sojourner Truth asked repeatedly, "Ain't I a woman?"*

---

*Nancy Skarmeas is a book editor and mother of a toddler, Gordon, who is keeping her and her husband quite busy at their home in New Hampshire. Her Greek and Irish ancestry has fostered a lifelong interest in research and history.*

# A Psalm
# of Thanksgiving

O COME, let us sing unto the Lord:
let us make a joyful noise
to the rock of our salvation.
Let us come before his presence
with thanksgiving,
and make a joyful noise
unto him with psalms.
For the Lord is a great God,
and a great King above all gods.
In his hand are the deep places
of the earth:
the strength of the hills is his also.
The sea is his, and he made it:
and his hands formed the dry land.
O come, let us worship and bow down:
let us kneel before the Lord our maker.
For he is our God;
and we are the people of his pasture,
and the sheep of his hand.

*Psalm 95:1–7*

*Vibrant maple trees surround a country church near Parfreyville, Wisconsin.*
*Photograph by Ken Dequaine.*

# FROM OF PLYMOUTH PLANTATION

*September 6, 1620.* Being thus arrived in a good harbor, and brought safe to land, they fell upon their knees and blessed the God of Heaven who had brought them over the vast and furious ocean, and delivered them from the perils and miseries thereof, again to set their feet on the firm and stable earth . . . Being thus passed the vast ocean, and a sea of troubles before in their preparation, they had now no friends to welcome them, nor inns to entertain or refresh their weather-beaten bodies, no houses or much less towns to repair to, to seek for succour. It is recorded in Scripture as a mercy to the Apostle and his shipwrecked company that the barbarians showed them no small kindness in refreshing them, but these savage barbarians, when they met with them, were readier to fill their sides full of arrows . . . And for the season it was winter, and they that know the winters of that country know them to be sharp and violent, and subject to cruel and fierce storms, dangerous to travel to known places, much more to search an unknown coast. Besides, what could they see but a hideous and desolate wilderness, full of wild beasts and wild men— and what multitudes there might be of them they knew not . . . Which way soever they turned their eyes (save upward to the heavens) they could have little solace or content in respect of any outward objects. For summer being done, all things stand upon them with a weather-beaten face, and the whole country, full of woods and thickets, represented a wild and savage hue. If they looked behind them, there was the mighty ocean they had passed and was now as a main bar and gulf to separate them from all the civil parts of the world . . .

What could now sustain them but the Spirit of God and His grace? May not and ought not the children of these fathers rightly say: "Our fathers were Englishmen which came over this great ocean and were ready to perish in this wilderness; but they cried unto the Lord, and He heard their voice and looked on their adversity. Let them therefore praise the Lord because He is good: and His mercies endure forever . . ."

*William Bradford*

---

## ABOUT THE TEXT

*In William Bradford's book,* Of Plymouth Plantation, *Bradford recounted the events that would later become monumental in our nation's history. With the aid of his journal, Bradford wrote a complete record of the Pilgrims' journey and the settlement of Plymouth colony. Bradford was a prominent figure in the voyage to America in 1620. His role as a leader continued with the building of the Plymouth colony, which also secured him the position as govenor for a total of thirty-three years. Despite his contribution as a political leader, Bradford is remembered more as a historian of those early years in American history.*

*Kelly LaSalle*

*Pilgrims gather together to give thanks and praise on* The First Thanksgiving Day. *Image from A. K. G., Berlin/Superstock.*

# THE CAPTAIN'S DAUGHTER

We were crowded in the cabin,
   Not a soul would dare to sleep, —
It was midnight on the waters,
   And a storm was on the deep.

'Tis a fearful thing in winter
   To be shattered by the blast,
And to hear the rattling trumpet
   Thunder, "Cut away the mast!"

So we shuddered there in silence, —
   For the stoutest held his breath,
While the hungry sea was roaring
   And the breakers talked with death.

As thus we sat in darkness,
   Each one busy with his prayers,
"We are lost!" the captain shouted,
   As he staggered down the stairs.

But his little daughter whispered,
   As she took his icy hand,
"Isn't God upon the ocean,
   Just the same as on the land?"

Then we kissed the little maiden,
   And we spake in better cheer,
And we anchored safe in harbor
   When the morn was shining clear.

*James Thomas Fields*

*Artist Robert W. Weir captures the prayerful attitude of America's
ancestors in The Embarcation of the Pilgrims. Image from Superstock.*

## A GOODWIFE'S CHRONICLE OF HER FIRST YEAR AT PLIMOUTH

After months at sea on *Mayflower*, we drop anchor in Plimouth Harbor. Our hopes soar. Surely here we will finally discover the liberty of mind and soul and body we desire. For here our leaders find a bay suitable for shipping, abounding with fish, eels and clams. The land is good for planting, crossed with streams of fresh water and near woods inhabited by wildlife. It seems an answer to our prayers. I know hopes must be tempered with reality for in our first year we will no doubt establish more than a new colony. We will establish the price of liberty and learn the preservance demanded by answered prayer.

When we set off for shore, the freezing winds drive our small shallop, stinging our faces and hands, crusting our coats with ice. It is December and we women and children remain aboard the *Mayflower* most of the time while the men cut trees and plane boards for building. The days are long and the children grow weary of confinement. One day Francis Billington and some other boys nearly destroy us all by shooting off a musket in the hold of the ship! Joy and sorrow mix. Mistress Susanna White is delivered of a healthy son she names Peregrine, the Wanderer. Shortly after this happy event, we are filled with grief when Elder Bradford's beloved wife Dorothy, falls overboard and drowns. I fear it is a pattern to be oft repeated through the year: joy and sorrow, birth and death.

By January we complete construction of the Common House where we store our provisions and ammunition. The hard work, freezing days and limited food supplies begin to take a toll on our citizens and many fall in. Sickbeds are set up in the Common House where the heat from fires gives warmth. Those of us well enough hunt, fish and care for the sick.

As the harsh winter continues into February, the sickness spreads. At times there are only six or seven of us well enough to tend the ill and bury the dead. Fearful that the Natives might learn how our numbers are decimated, we dig our graves at night and leave them unmarked. One day a spark from the chimney sets the thatched roof of the Common House afire. With haste we carry out the sick and drag provisions away from the burning building. In the end the fire is stilled and repairs made, but spirits sag and only our faith in God carries us through the dark time we name "The Great Sickness."

By March, our numbers are down by half to fifty-one souls. Those of us left take in the children orphaned in the plague, comforted in our own losses by their need of loving care. The sickness abates and the weather turns warm renewing our hope. Encouraged by the Lord and one another we dare to believe we can survive in this new land after all. This hope is confirmed by the arrival of two new friends: Samoset and Squanto. These Natives know English, and introduce our leaders to their great sagamore, or chief, Massasoit. Captain Standish and Master Williamson, aided by Squanto, draft a treaty of mutual benefit with Massasoit and thus make peace with our neighbors.

With safety secured and Spring's return our little settlement comes to life again. Squanto is an invaluable friend, teaching us the secrets of living from the land and sea. Following his direction, we plant fields of corn, peas, and beans and learn to catch the abundant alewives and bass in the bay; however, none of us has attained his skill in catching eels with our bare hands! There are changes all about us and in our community as well. Governor John Carver dies suddenly after coming from the fields complaining of severe head pains. Soon after, Elder William Bradford is elected to succeed him. When the *Mayflower* weighs anchor to set sail for England on April 5th, not one Pilgrim chooses to leave our new home. It is surprising that with all the hardship, we remain committed. The Lord stands firm and so do we.

Wildflowers and herbs cover the forest floor and meadows near the settlement. There is a freshness in the air and the promise of our dreams fulfilled.

Edward Winslow and the Widow Susanna White are married in our first civil ceremony. It is another beginning for us all and we dare to look to the future.

We commence building cabins for individual families. After months in the Common House, we are anxious to have a bit more privacy and independence. The men also make plans to build a fort on the high ground at the end of the settlement. We will hold Sunday services and meetings there as well. The months of June and July are busy as we tend our crops and construct our homes.

In early August, Johnny Billington wanders off into the woods. He and his brothers are such troublemakers that some in the community believe we should consider his absence a blessing. Christian charity, however, overrules and a search party sets out. After several days they discover Johnny adorned with feathers and beads, having a good time with our Indian neighbors. They do not seem reluctant to return him.

By fall our little plantation boasts seven family homes and four structures for common use. We work together two weeks to bring in the harvest God has granted from our twenty acres of Indian corn and six acres of barley, beans, and peas. Cod, bass, and other fish are dried and stored as well as waterfowl and venison. We shall not starve this winter as we nearly did the last.

The year has come full circle and we gather to give thanks to God, joined by our Indian friends. Both God and they have blessed us with encouragement when our own strength faltered. It has been a hard year, but all that is worthwhile is purchased with a price. Our efforts are a small beginning in so great a land, yet our hearts are enlarged with gratitude as we consider all that God has provided. In years hence perhaps others will remember us and gain courage to seek their own liberty, confident in the knowledge that true freedom is never truly free.

---

*Pamela Kennedy is a freelance writer of short stories, articles, essays, and children's books. Wife of a retired naval officer and mother of three children, she has made her home on both U.S. coasts and currently resides in Kent, Washington.*

# A THANKSGIVING

For the wealth of pathless forests,
Whereon no axe may fall;
For the winds that haunt the branches;
The young bird's timid call;
For the red leaves dropped like rubies
Upon the dark green sod;
For the waving of the forests—
    I thank thee, O my God!

For the sound of waters gushing
In bubbling beads of light;
For the fleets of snow-white lilies
Firm-anchored out of sight;
For the reeds among the eddies;
The crystal on the clod;
For the flowing of the rivers—
    I thank Thee, O my God!

For the rosebud's break of beauty
Along the toiler's way;
For the violet's eye that opens
To bless the new-born day;
For the bare twigs that in summer
Bloom like the prophet's rod;
For the blossoming of flowers—
    I thank Thee, O my God!

For the lifting up of mountains
In brightness and in dread;
For the peaks where snow and sunshine
Alone have dared to tread;
For the dark of silent gorges,
Whence mighty cedars nod;
For the majesty of mountains—
    I thank Thee, O my God!

For the splendor of the sunsets
Vast mirrored on the sea;
For the gold fringed clouds, that curtain
Heaven's inner mystery;
For the molten bars of twilight,
Where thought leans, glad, yet awed,
For the glory of the sunsets—
    I thank Thee, O my God!

For the earth, and all its beauty;
The sky, and all its light;
For the dim and soothing shadows
That rest the dazzled sight;
For unfading fields and prairies,
Where sense in vain has trod;
For the world's exhaustless beauty—
    I thank Thee, O my God!

For an eye of inward seeing;
A soul to know and love;
For these common aspirations,
That our high heirship prove;
For the hearts that bless each other
Beneath Thy smile, Thy rod;
For the amaranth saved from Eden—
    I thank Thee, O my God!

For the hidden scroll, o'erwritten
With one dear Name adored;
For the Heavenly in the human;
The Spirit in the Word;
For the tokens of Thy presence
Within, above, abroad;
For Thine own great gift of Being—
    I thank Thee, O my God!

*Lucy Larcom*

*Matthiessen Falls flow through the colorful forest of the Upper Dells in Matthiessen State Park, Illinois. Photograph by Terry Donnelly.*

## I WILL GO WITH MY FATHER A-PLOUGHING

I will go with my father a-ploughing
To the **green** field by the sea,
And the rooks and corbies and seagulls
Will come flocking after me.
I will sing to the patient horses
With the lark in the shine of the air,
And my father will sing the plough-song
That blesses the cleaving share.

I will go with my father a-sowing
To the **red** field by the sea,
And the merls and robins and thrushes
Will come flocking after me.
I will sing to the striding sowers
With the finch on the flowering sloe,
And my father will sing the seed-song
That only the wise men know.

I will go with my father a-reaping
To the **brown** field by the sea,
And the geese and pigeons and sparrows
Will come flocking after me.
I will sing to the weary reapers
With the wren in the heat of the sun,
And my father will sing the scythe-song
That joys for the harvest done.

*Joseph Campbell*

*American artist Donald Zolan captures the helpful spirit of a young farm boy
in Too Busy to Play. © Zolan Fine Arts, Ltd. Hershey, Pennsylvania.*

# I Love a Windy Day

I love a windy day, when breezes run
Like throngs of happy children in the sun.
Their feet swirl playful eddies in the grass,
They tag each leaf and petal as they pass.
And overhead, with romping energy,
They send clouds scudding like white sails at sea.

My heart goes dancing with a lightfoot breeze;
We do a do-si-do above the trees.
And soon vexations have been wafted higher
Than weathercocks upon the tallest spire.
I whisk through all my work at double pace,
While joy pirouettes in smiles across my face.

Gail Brook Burket

*Wheat fields ready for harvest wave in the breeze in Palouse, Washington.
Photograph by Gene Ahrens/H. Armstrong Roberts.*

*A cornhusk teacher doll holds her miniature chalkboard up for all to see.*
*Photograph by Dennis Thompson/Unicorn Stock Photos.*

## CORNHUSK DOLLS
*McKenna Denver*

A few years ago, a dairy farm in our small town went the way of too many family farms and sold off its cows and stopped producing milk. But this family was luckier than most. The farm had been profitable for many generations and the family was financially secure; so instead of selling off their land to developers, they transformed the cow pastures into hay fields and a thriving, large-scale vegetable garden. They even outfitted the cow barn as an ice-cream stand, a produce market, and a showcase for local craftspeople. The house remains home to three generations of the family, and the barnyard has become a perfect little petting farm with lambs, piglets, goats, and a thirty-year-old pony. A weekly visit to this old farm is a cherished ritual in our family—a summer outing we cling to well into autumn, as close to the October 31 closing date as the weather will allow.

This year on our final visit, after a gooey hot fudge sundae, I browsed the craft shop while my husband took the little ones around for a last hello to the animals. In a corner of the shop, as part of an autumn display, I noticed something I hadn't seen before—adorable cornhusk dolls with calico aprons in the most beautiful fall colors. Thinking ahead to Thanksgiving, when I would have six little nieces and nephews under the age of five at my table, I purchased enough of these dolls to mark each child's place at the table—a little surprise to make the day special.

The kids loved the dolls—proof of what we parents all know but sometimes forget: it is often the simplest things that delight our children the most. After dinner, while they played, my eldest niece asked if I had made the cornhusk dolls. I told her no, and when I noticed she looked a bit disappointed, I told her I thought they might be easy to make and maybe we could try. Since they were at our house for the weekend, we decided to head to the craft store the next morning for supplies and see what we could find. We brought home a pile of dried cornhusks—drying our own would take too long and summer corn was already long past season—and two colors of fabric, along with some chestnut brown yarn to use as hair. I even found a craft book with some helpful instructions and background information on working with cornhusks.

Cornhusk dolls represent a borrowed tradition from the culture of the Native Americans. Since corn was a staple crop among the Native Americans, husks (also called corn shucks) were plentiful after the harvest. With the later tradition of the husking bee (a social occasion for rural families to gather together to husk the corn and celebrate the harvest), husks were often saved by the women and reserved for doll-making. I was delighted to have the opportunity to teach my niece a little about our own American history as we learned together about this harvest craft.

This is a wonderful project for little hands. There are no special tools required, not much cutting or measuring, and precision is not necessary. The husks are wrapped and tied to form a body, arms, and a head; and the bottom can be made as a skirt or as two legs. Eyes can be added with a felt tip pen, yarn glued in place for hair, and the fabric aprons made as simply or as detailed as you like. The husks are soaked in warm water before use to make them supple, and take only a couple of hours to dry after the doll is completed. Our instructions were easy enough for my niece to follow as I read them. Cornhusks have one side that is smooth and the other side is ribbed. For our dolls, we choose to use the ribbed side of the corn husks as the "right" side. While we left our husks in their natural color, the husks can be dyed very effectively with fabric dye. Look in craft books at the library or a local shop—especially those about folk art—for guidance in creating your own cornhusk dolls.

The dolls I made with my niece are just as charming as those I bought in the craft shop—less perfect in form but lovingly made. I have resolved that next summer I will save my own cornhusks and dry them in the sun. Then, at Thanksgiving time, I will have the materials on hand. My niece says that next year she will show my daughter, only three years old now, how to make a doll. I hope that she will; and maybe in years to come, my daughter can show some of her younger cousins. It can be challenging to have a house full of kids on a cold November weekend; and it can be even harder to get the little ones' attention with all their toys, classes, and videos. But this year, in the guise of these simple dolls, we found something to brighten the little ones' day and bring us all just a little closer together.

# MANITOU'S GARDEN

"Come, play in my garden!"
　　Called flaxen-haired Fred,
Peeping out from the edge
　　Of a hyacinth-bed
Through the stout oaken rails,
　　At a Chippewa boy
Who ran along dragging
　　A snake, for a toy.

"I'll give you some flowers
　　To twist in your hair."

"The son of a sachem
　　No blossoms will wear
That the white man has planted;
　　Nor yet will he go
Where roses and lilies
　　Like pale captives grow.

"In Manitou's garden
　　Are gay flowers to see:
Come out, little pale-face,
　　And play here with me!
The fawn will play with us,—
　　The squirrel and the hare;
No fences to stop us,—
　　We're free as the air.

"In Manitou's garden
　　How bright is the dawn!
We know where his trail
　　Through the deer-path has gone.
The moccasin-flower

Springs up where he stopped;
And the dewdrops are beads,
    From his blanket's edge dropped."

"I'm afraid, little Indian,
    To come out to you.
I'm afraid of the snakes
    And the barking wolves too."

"Ugh! white-hearted pale-face,
    They're Manitou's snakes,
And the wolves are the hounds
    That a-hunting he takes.

"We too on wild mustangs
    Chase bison and deer.
We are Manitou's hunters,
    A race without fear.
Our arrow's flight leaves
    The swift eagle behind.
Whoop! after them, quick
    As the rushing north-wind!"

But the son of the Chippewa
    Stands there alone,
At his whoop timid Fred
    To his mother has flown.
Off the red boy runs, shouting,
    "Whoop! whoop! let him be!
In Manitou's garden
    Are playmates for me!"

*Lucy Larcom*

# BALSAM
# PILLOW

I slept on a balsam pillow
And dreamed of woods and streams
And heard the meadowlark's clear call
Piping through my dreams.
And the muted sound of water leaping
Ran like gay music through my sleeping.

I slept on a balsam pillow
And the northern woods were mine
And I felt the wind in my tired heart,
Blowing o'er fir and pine,
And the smell of the wild was sweet to the taste
Of brown clean waters and marshy waste.

I slept on a balsam pillow,
Far from the haunts of men,
And the smoke from a campfire drifted by,
Sweet in my face again.
And I heard the hoot-owl's mournful cry,
And the wings of wild geese going by.

I slept on a balsam pillow
And the smell of the earth was sweet,
Needles of pine like a Persian rug
Spongy beneath my feet.
The taste of resin and sage and brier,
Ashes blown from a woodland fire.

*Edna Jaques*

*Snow sprinkles aspens and evergreens in the Maroon Creek Canyon of
White River National Forest, Colorado. Photograph by Jeff Gnass Photography.*

# The Wings of the Morning

These, the Wings of the Morning,
An Indian Maiden wove,
Intertwining subtilely
Wands from a willow grove
Beside the Sangamon—

Rude stream of Dreamland Town.
She bound them to my shoulders
With fingers golden-brown.
The wings were part of me;
The willow-wands were hot.
Pulses from my heart
Healed each bruise and spot
Of the morning-glory buds,
Beginning to unfold
Beneath her burning song of suns untold.

*Vachel Lindsay*

**Sweet** is the breath of morn;
her rising sweet with charm
of earliest birds.

*John Milton*

# COLLECTOR'S

# NAVAJO BLANKETS

by Emily York

More than one guest in my home has asked about the three Navajo blankets that decorate my living room walls. They want to know where they came from, who made them, and more than anything else, how I came to have three beautiful examples of Southwestern Native American art on the walls of my rustic northern New Hampshire farmhouse. I guess I can understand their question. Objectively, the Navajo blankets seem out of place amidst the hand-hewn ceiling beams, the wide-plank pine floors, the braided wool rug, and the collection of antique furnishings which, while certainly eclectic, have an unmistakable flavor of New England. I have never been much concerned with decorating by themes or specific styles, however; and to me, my Navajo blankets exist in my home in perfect harmony.

My modest collection of Navajo blankets was born thirty-five years ago when my grandfather, a widower who had taken up traveling to ease his loneliness, brought two blankets home from a trip to New Mexico—one for me and one for my younger sister. We grew up thinking of Papa as a true adventurer, for he had traveled all around the world several times over and always came home full of stories of faraway places. I was ten years old when Papa brought home that blanket; I had only infrequently left the small village where we lived and had only once set foot outside the state of New Hampshire, that being for a trip down to Boston to visit an ailing aunt. The blanket—just like all of

This Navajo pictorial blanket dates back to the 1890s.
Image from the Lowe Art Museum,
The University of Miami/Superstock.

Papa's postcards, gifts, and stories—brought a thrilling hint of the great wide world into our little country home. I hung on to that blanket through all of the changes in my life to come, even when I had had enough travels and adventures of my own to make it seem less exotic.

Papa's blanket is tightly woven of undyed wools in a simple pattern of browns, blacks, grays, and soft whites, and its warmth and smell still bring Papa to mind.

When I was thirty years old, I visited the Southwest for myself and bought my own Navajo blanket. This one is quite different than the one Papa brought home. It was woven in the 1890s, during a period when Navajo weavers gave in to the demands of customers and began incorporating Turkish and Persian rug designs into their blankets. This one was actually made to be used as a rug, but I rescued it from that fate and have always called it a blanket. I did not decide to hang the blankets on the walls, however, until after I brought home the third member of my collection—one purchased in New York City, of all places. I bought it in a little shop that dealt in Southwestern and Native American art. The woman there told me that it represented a low point in Navajo weaving, a time when the old techniques were compromised by consumer demand. In addition to the undyed colors found in my first two rugs, this one features machine spun yarns in reds and golds and oranges. It is less tightly woven than the other, and thus less durable, but still handmade and impressive. Even when the Navajo weavers compromised their art, they remained skilled craftswomen and inspired artists.

So how did these blankets end up on my wall? When we moved into this house a few years ago, I was looking for something to hang in my living room between the windows that look out into our front yard and across the old pasture on the other side of the road. The blankets just seemed right. They remind me of Papa, gone now, and of all the happy times I had listening his stories of adventure. And, to be honest, I don't see them as out of place at all. Today, as I sit by the front windows and look out on the blazing golds and reds of our two ancient sugar maples, the blankets beside the windows provide a complementary frame. But it even goes beyond that. My rustic old house may be classically New England, but it was built on the universal principle of practicality. Two hundred years ago, our house was actually a barn. When that farm family's son wanted a house of his own,

the old barn was transformed into a house—a two-room home with a central fireplace and a sleeping loft for the son and his new wife. In years to come, a couple of small additions were added and the sleeping loft was transformed into two bedrooms. That's how we found the house a few years ago, and we've been working on our own additions and improvements. I may not be objective, but I think that old barn has become quite a charming house—the practical made beautiful. Which brings me back to the blankets. Centuries ago, maybe about the time when the first rafters of the old barn were raised, Navajo women wove blankets to keep them warm at night. They made the blankets beautiful with color and design and the skill of their hands at the loom. Today, nearly a continent and several lifetimes away, three of these blankets have found a new, but still practical use—they add beauty and harmony to my home.

# WRAPPED IN A COLORFUL HISTORY

*If you would like to begin collecting Navajo blankets, here are some interesting facts:*

## HISTORY

• Navajo women have been weaving for more than three centuries. Traditionally, they've woven blankets, which were used as bed coverings, dresses, and doorway coverings. It was in response to non-Navajo consumer demand in the 1800s that Navajo women began to weave rugs.

• Navajo legend tells of a goddess called Spider Woman who taught the first Navajo women the art of weaving. Custom calls for spider webs to be rubbed on the hands of infant Navajo girls so that Spider Woman will one day teach them to weave.

• Before 1870, Navajo women wove blankets from hand-spun, undyed wool in white, gray, brown, tan, and black. These blankets were tightly woven and used traditional Navajo motifs in their designs; no two designs were identical.

• Between 1875 and 1890, synthetic dyes and machine-spun dyes came into use. Increased demand from outside the Navajo community caused weavers to increase production; the result is many blankets that are loosely woven and of an inferior quality in comparison to earlier pieces.

• After 1890, Navajo women began to incorporate Persian rug designs into their weaving at the

request of buyers from around the world. They also returned to the former style of dense and tightly woven blankets, because much of their weaving was now being used as floor coverings.

• By the 1920s, Navajo women reclaimed their old styles and techniques and began producing blankets in the centuries-old manner.

• Proof of the durability of Navajo weaving came at the 1933 Chicago World's Fair. A Navajo rug marked the entrance to the New Mexico hall; an estimated three million pairs of feet walked over the rug during the fair. When it was taken up and inspected, not a thread was out of place.

• Navajo blankets were traditionally woven in three sizes. The largest, the men's blankets, were 50 x 70 inches. Slightly smaller were the women's blankets, used as bed coverings and also as wrap dresses. The smallest were the children's blankets.

## DESIGNS

• Pictorial rugs show modern reservation scenes.

• Teec Nos Pos rugs incorporate Persian designs along with traditional Navajo motifs

• The Two Grey Hills design features undyed wools in brown, tan, black, and white.

# HARVEST
# FIELD

The cornfield has its hair on end
    As if afraid of ghosts tonight.
Along the stubble, pumpkin suns
    Reflect last rays of autumn light.

A ground hog waddles into his hole,
    Its entrance dry and summer worn.
Startled, a rabbit with button tail
    Whisks behind a shock of corn.

And post-rail dining, one gray squirrel
    Removes fat kernels from a husk,
While time-defying hills beyond
    Are brushed away by feathered dusk.

*Gertrude Ryder Bennett*

*At this family farm in Chester, Vermont, harvested pumpkins await transformation into jack-o'-lanterns. Photograph by William Johnson/Johnson's Photography*

# Cornfields

When on the breath of Autumn's breeze,
    From pastures dry and brown,
Goes floating, like an idle thought,
    The fair, white thistle-down, —
Oh, then what joy to walk at will
    Upon the golden harvest-hill!

What joy in dreaming ease to lie
    Amid a field new shorn;
And see all round, on sunlit slopes,
    The piled-up shocks of corn;
And send the fancy wandering o'er
    All pleasant harvest-fields of yore!

I feel the day; I see the field;
    The quivering of the leaves;
And good old Jacob and his horse, —
    Binding the yellow sheaves!
And at this very hour I seem
    To be with Joseph in his dream!

I see the fields of Bethlehem
    And reapers many a one
Bending unto their sickles' stroke,

And Boaz looking on;
And Ruth, the Moabitess fair,
    Among the gleaners stooping there!

Again, I see a little child,
    His mother's sole delight, —
God's living gift of love unto
    The kind, good Shunamite;
To mortal pangs I see him yield,
    And the lad bear him from the field.

The sun-bathed quiet of the hills,
    The fields of Galilee,
That eighteen hundred years ago
    Were full of corn, I see;
And the dear Saviour take his way
    Mid ripe ears on the Sabbath-day.

Oh, golden fields of bending corn,
    How beautiful they seem!
The reaper-folk, the piled-up sheaves,
    To me are like a dream;
The sunshine and the very air
    Seem of old time and take me there!

                      Mary Howitt

Corn shocks bask in the golden glow of sunset in the Blue Ridge Mountains of North Carolina. Photograph by William Johnson/Johnson's Photography.

# MOUNTAIN MEASURE

I shall remember this when Time grows old:
Our campfire blazing by a mountain stream,
The Rockies towering into skies of gold,
And dark pines tall against a sunset dream.
Blue smoke will rise through all my memories
With fragrance of this Colorado night,
And silhouettes of sturdy alpine trees
Will stand forever through a city's light.
And if the Rockies lift their lofty peaks
Beyond our human reach, the heart can share
Something of majesty. The thing it seeks
Will grow in recognition as we dare.
Mountains will measure, as we feel our part,
The smallness or the greatness of the heart.

*Mary E. Linton*

*Even in autumn the Maroon Bells in the Rocky Mountain National Park of Colorado are dusted with snow. Photograph by Dick Dietrich.*

## from A LADY'S LIFE IN THE ROCKY MOUNTAINS
### Isabella Bird (1831–1904)

As we crept from the Ledge round a horn of rock, I beheld what made me perfectly sick and dizzy to look at—the terminal Peak itself—a smooth, cracked face or wall of pink granite, as nearly perpendicular as anything could well be up which it was possible to climb, well deserving the name of the "American Matterhorn."

*Scaling*, not climbing, is the correct term for this last ascent. It took one hour to accomplish 500 feet, pausing for breath every minute or two. The only foothold was in narrow cracks or on minute projections of the granite. To get a toe in these cracks, or here and there on a scarcely oblivious projection, while crawling on hands and knees, all the while tortured with thirst and gasping and struggling for breath, this was the climb; but at last the Peak was won. A grand, well-defined mountain-top it is, a nearly level acre of boulders, with precipitous sides all round, the one we came up being the only accessible one.

It was not possible to remain long. One of the young men was seriously alarmed by bleeding from the lungs, and the intense dryness of the day and the rarefaction of the air, at a height of nearly 15,000 feet, made respiration very painful. There is always water on the Peak, but it was frozen as hard as a rock, and the sucking of ice and snow increases thirst. We all suffered severely from the want of water, and the gasping for breath made our mouths and tongues so dry that articulation was difficult, and the speech of all unnatural.

From the summit were seen in the unrivalled combination all the views which had rejoined our eyes during the ascent. It was something at last to stand upon the storm-rent crown of this lonely sentinel of the Rocky Range, on one of the mightiest of the vertebrae of the backbone of the North American continent, and to see the waters start for both oceans. Uplifted above love and hate and storms of passion, calm amidst the eternal silences, fanned by zephyrs and bathed in living blue, peace rested for that one bright day on the Peak, as if it were some region

Where falls not rain, or hail, or any snow,
Or ever wind blows loudly.

---

*Under doctor's orders, Isabella Bird (1831–1904) began traveling at age forty to ease her bad back and insomnia. She took the prescription seriously and kept traveling for the next thirty plus years until her death. Bird traveled to places as far away as Japan and Tibet and as close to the heart of America as the Rocky Mountains. It was in the Rockies that Bird wrote the delightful letters to her sister Henrietta that later became the collection entitled,* A Lady's Life in the Rocky Mountains. *Bird made great strides for women adventurers through her travels and writings; in 1893 she became the first woman to address the members of the Royal Geographical Society.*

*Morning light breaks on Ohio Creek Valley and the Rocky Mountains in Gunnison National Forest, Colorado. Photograph by Terry Donnelly.*

# GIFT OF THE SNOWGEESE

One memorable autumn night several years ago, I heard eerie noises outside my cottage, which was situated beside a small cove of a large Missouri lake.

So at three A.M., robe-clad, I tiptoed out alone into the brisk, starry night to investigate. When I reached the water's edge, my eyes took in the sight of hundreds of snow geese. They ruffled their feathers as they searched for a place to settle in this sheltering cove, where they would spend one night of rest after what must have been an arduous day of flight on the journey to their southern, winter's haven.

As if programmed by some great, divine computer eons ago, the snow geese now swayed and flowed together with no struggle for dominance over one another. In a remarkable show of group self-discipline, not a single utterance came forth—a show of solidarity amidst the threat of night predators. Unavoidably, the air was dominated by an almost roaring "whoosh" from the multitude of wings and downy feathers adjusting to the water and from the crowding together of mated-for-life parents, cozying for the night with their offspring.

The cove and the night air gave a sonority and power to the strange flutterings. The moon was in absolute fullness, making the vision before me as clear as daylight. The water shimmered lavishly with lunar reflections, while the satiny-white, floating bodies appeared as one huge, luminous mass of unity and harmony.

Breathing the clear air into my lungs, I stood enraptured with awe and reverence for a long time, how long I will never know. It was almost as if time stood still. Then softly, slowly, a blanket of stillness and peace descended upon this cove of rest.

Standing in the hush, I felt as if these lovely creatures had given me the gift of their presence. I had witnessed a chapter in the mysterious phenomenon of life known as "migration." The chances of being there at that moment and at that place were so very slim; it was a marvel to have seen that particular, rarely-encountered species at all. And in what remarkable circumstances! The entire event could have been so easily missed or ignored, the way so many things are. How many and how often, most of us may never know, but the event of that wondrous night has caused me to be ever more aware and in tune to the possibility of hearing that next "rustle of wings and feathers," calling me to respond to another experience of exquisite beauty and peace.

*Phyllis Hensel Smith*

*A flock of snow geese journey together along the eastern shore of Maryland. Photograph by Superstock.*

# Frost-Blossom

The tree has blossomed overnight,
For every twig is frozen white
And garlanded with crystal sprays
That sparkle in the sun's bright rays.

Each sprig is tipped with buds of rime,
Strange burgeonings of Wintertime—
As lovely as a Spring display
Of plum and damson, pear and may.

And on the window I can trace,
Where silver branches interlace,
A picture on the pane embossed:
A fairy orchard white with frost.

*Patience Strong*

*A red maple leaf nestles in the sheltering branches
of a snowy fir tree. Photograph by Superstock.*

# Readers' Forum

*Snapshots from Our Ideals Readers*

ABOVE: Marie Dawson of Baltimore, Maryland, sent us this picture of her great-grandaughter, Gabrielle Marie Benson. This picture of little one-year-old Gabrielle is entitled "Find the Baby" by her Great-Grandmother. Gabrielle's parents, Donald and Shannon Benson, took the picture in honor of their daughter's first visit to the pumpkin farm. Marie is delighted that she has the opportunity of seeing Gabrielle almost every day and says that her great-grandaughter is a very happy and friendly little girl.

ABOVE: Six-month-old Sarah Ann Meeusen beams brightly in her new dress for church. Sarah's great-grandmother, Mary Masten of Mesa, Arizona, wanted to share this picture with the *Ideals* family of readers. Sarah lives with her parents, James and Kimberly Meeusen, along with her three older brothers in Kimmel Surprize, Arizona. Mary describes Sarah as "all smiles" and "full of fun." Sarah's grandmother, Sonny Conley of La Cruces, New Mexico, took this snapshot of Sarah.

THANK YOU Marie Dawson and Mary Masten for sharing your family photographs with *Ideals*. We hope to hear from other readers who would like to share snapshots with the *Ideals* family. Please include a self-addressed, stamped envelope if you would like the photos returned. Keep your original photographs for safekeeping and send duplicate photos along with your name, address, and telephone number to:

READERS' FORUM
IDEALS PUBLICATIONS INC.
P.O. BOX 305300
NASHVILLE, TENNESSEE 37230

**Publisher**, Patricia A. Pingry

**Editor**, Lisa C. Ragan

**Prepress Manager**, Eve DeGrie

**Editorial Assistant**, Andrea Zywicki

**Editorial Intern**, Kelly LaSalle

**Contributing Editors**, Lansing Christman, Deana Deck, Pamela Kennedy, Patrick McRae, Nancy Skarmeas

ACKNOWLEDGMENTS

BALSAM PILLOW from ROSES IN DECEMBER by Edna Jacques. Copyright © in Canada by Thomas Allen & Son Limited. Reprinted with the permission of Adventure Publications. AUTUMN IN TENNESSEE and SIGN POSTS from AGAINST ALL TIME by Isla Paschal Richardson. Reprinted with permission of Branden Publishing Co. THE SHEAVES from THE COLLECTED POEMS OF EDWIN ARLINGTON ROBINSON by E. A. Robinson. Reprinted with the permission of Simon & Schuster. Copyright © 1925 by Macmillan Publishing Company, renewed 1953 by Ruth Nivison and Barbara R. Holt. FROST BLOSSOM from MAGIC CASEMENTS by Patience Strong. Reprinted with the permission of Rupert Crew Limited, London. Our sincere thanks to the following authors whom we were unable to contact: Josephine Powell Beaty for OCTOBER; Gertrude Ryder Bennett for HARVEST FIELD; Reid Crowell for A FARMER REMEMBERS; May Smith White for AUTUMN'S GOLDEN HOUR.

## HOME AGAIN

It's grand to go on holiday
    And break the set routine.
It is nice to get away
    And have a change of scene.
It's a tonic, so they say,

To see and to explore—
The exciting world that starts outside
    Your own front door.

But there comes the moment when
    You've had enough of it.
Then it's home you long for—
    That's the corner where you fit.
The spot where you can be yourself.
    It calls you from afar:
Your own small, cozy kingdom
    Where you know just where you are.

When you think you're in a groove
    You feel you'd like to see—
Other places, other faces, other company.
    But oh, it's good to get
Back home and breathe your native air—
    And to settle down into
        Your own familiar chair.

*Patience Strong*